IMAGES
of England

KNOTTINGLEY AND FERRYBRIDGE

The Carter family take a walk in the grounds of Lime Grove in the 1880s.

IMAGES
of England

KNOTTINGLEY AND FERRYBRIDGE

Compiled by
Wendy Bellwood
on behalf of
Wakefield Metropolitan District
Library & Information Services

TEMPUS

First published 1999
Copyright © Wakefield Metropolitan District
Library & Information Services, 1999

Tempus Publishing Limited
The Mill, Brimscombe Port,
Stroud, Gloucestershire, GL5 2QG

ISBN 0 7524 1564 6

Typesetting and origination by
Tempus Publishing Limited
Printed in Great Britain by
Midway Clark Printing, Wiltshire

The Marshes, Knottingley.

Cattle grazing on the marshes at the turn of the century.

Contents

Acknowledgements

This book would not have been possible without the help and support of in particular:
Mr W. Askin, Peter Cookson, Denise Cusworth, Mr B. Gosney, Ron Gosney, Mr P. Greenwood,
Mr D. Hall, Wendy Jewitt, Mrs M. Langton, Mr W. Lyon, Maud Photographic Studios, Mr G.
Norton, Mr H. Pickard, Graham Stokes, Julie Travis, Richard Van Riel (museum services), Sue
Wiggins, Mr W.E. Wilson, Mrs W. Wright.

I would also like to thank everyone else who offered advice, help and support.

Mary Lightowler in her trap, driving 'Queenie' in the early 1930s.

Introduction

This book was written in an attempt to record the many facets of Knottingley and Ferrybridge. Dating back to a Saxon settlement on the banks of the River Aire, Knotttingley has constantly changed and adapted. The changes over the last hundred years have been immense and the town we know today bears little resemblance to the Knottingley of old.

In 1892 the town was described in a trade directory as having the churches of St Botolph and Christ Church, Wesleyan, Primitive Methodist and Congregational chapels, a Red Ribbon tabernacle in Cow Lane and a Salvation Army Barracks in Chapel Street. By 1884 the vicar of St Botolph's was complaining that the Red Ribbon Club was hindering his work by baptizing children, who would formerly have been baptized in church, at the low charge of six pence per child. A cemetery of about four acres, which contained two mortuary chapels, was opened in 1858 and the Local Board acted as a Burial Board.

At this time there were four shipbuilding yards, along with maltings, mills, potteries, roperies, limekilns, tar works, glass bottle works, an extensive brewery, and earthenware manufacturers. The public offices included a police sergeant, deputy coroner, medical officer, public vaccinator, registrars for marriages and also births and deaths and the Pontefract union. A surveyor and Inspector of Nuisances and collector of rates were employed along with a bill poster, and a lodging house was situated at Hill Top. The post office was also an annuity and insurance office and a carrier delivered to Pontefract four times each week. Travel was possible by coach, boat and railway. The industries listed also include iron and brass founders, a gas works, a printer and stationer, a threshing mill, chemical manure manufacturers, tar distillers, a steam saw mill and a ship's tackle maker. Interestingly one of the occupations listed is that of a willow grower; the willow would probably have been used to make baskets for the transportation of glass and ceramics.

In Aire Street alone, the following were listed: drapers, coal dealers, chemists and druggists, carpenters, carters and hauliers, boot and shoe makers, a chimney sweep, bakers, a basket maker, solicitors, dressmakers, tailors, milliners, fishmongers, grocers, shopkeepers, greengrocers, hairdressers, joiners, plumbers and glaziers, a saddler, a watch and clock maker, a hosier, a metal worker, wine and spirit merchant, a wool and fancy repository, an earthenware dealer, a wardrobe dealer and a seedsman.

The industries in and around the area were immensely diverse and ranged between shipbuilding, glassmaking, pottery manufacture, lime quarrying, brewing and even electric blanket manufacturing. This diversity was made possible due to the unique physical location of the town.

The once bustling shopping area of Aire Street and Chapel Street has disappeared to be replaced by housing, and the large private dwellings of local industrialists no longer exist. Knottingley Carnival is still an annual event, dating back to the first carnival in 1932, and its predecessor 'Infirmary Sunday'. The last seventy years have seen the power station at Ferrybridge rebuilt three times and, most notably, the spectacular collapse of the cooling towers of Ferrybridge C in September 1968.

The section of photographs entitled Dakky's were all taken by a travelling photographer who processed his own photographs in a wooden hut on the banks of the canal. He toured the area taking photographs of local groups and events and added his own captions to them.

The purpose of this book for the future is to publicize the photographs already available and encourage the gathering together of a collection of photographs at Knottingley Library which will ensure that present and future generations will have as complete a visual record of the town's past as possible. We hope to remind everyone that the photographs of 'ordinary' people are a valuable heritage for the history of an area and an evocative reminder of times past. A heritage that should be preserved and available for all to see.

Wendy Bellwood
March 1999

One

Changing Town

Views from a series of postcards of Knottingley produced in the 1950s.

People stand outside the cottages at Hill Top, in the early 1900s. They are looking down from Goal Yard. This is currently the site of the post office.

Looking down Hill Top from the top of Forge Hill Lane. The pub on the right is the Bay Horse which, in 1837, was run by William Taylor. The building situated almost centrally is the old Co-op.

Hill Top, showing the site of the present traffic lights, early this century. The shop on the right is Clayton's Grocers; the old Commercial pub is the closest building. On the left is Carter's Square. Kelly's directory for 1892 lists a 'Railway Family and Commercial Hotel' at Hill Top whose proprietor was Joseph Clements.

Hill Top, c. 1950. The buildings on the right have since been replaced by an arcade of shops and banks.

Ropewalk in the early 1900s. In Knottingley several ropewalks existed to produce the rope required in the shipping industry. In 1892 Mary Jane Howard produced ropes at Grove House and David Kellett was in production at Shepherd's Bridge. Ropewalk also boasted a Gentleman's Club in 1892.

The building changes can be seen here in the 1920s. To make sure that ropes were not stolen strands of coloured rope were introduced into the design, so that it was possible to tell where a rope had been manufactured.

A terrace of houses at 'Long Row' or 'Gaping Row', possibly just before demolition. The correct name was Jacksonville. The sports centre now occupies this site.

A rural scene of Manor Farm with St Botolph's church in the background, in the 1950s. This is the oldest domestic building in the town and it is reputed that the last bull-baiting in England was held here. Bull-baiting was outlawed by Parliament in 1823.

A lorry makes a delivery at Womersley Road in the 1950s.

Racca Green, in the 1950s. In 1892 Miss Thwaites and Mrs Senior are listed as private residents at Racca Green, with Richard Hey running his business as a lime burner there as well. Racca Green in 1892 also boasted an Inspector of Nuisances and a cow keeper in residence.

Shepherds Bridge with Bridge Court on the left, in the 1950s. The houses on the right are now part of Gregg's glassworks. Over the bridge on the left corner is Braims' butcher shop.

The entrance to Gregg's glassworks with a group of workers just visible.

The exit from the Greenhouse playing fields onto Glebe Lane. Extensive glebe lands were attached to Knottingley, the revenue from which was intended to be used for repairs to the church.

The Greenhouse playing fields in the early 1900s. The land was purchased from Mr Jackson, the money being raised by a 'mile of pennies' and wage deductions. The drinking fountain is situated in a recess on the right.

Ernest Hague, schoolmaster and organist at St Botolph's church. Known as 'Daddy' Hague he was also responsible for organizing the drama group.

St Botolph's church in the 1950s. St Botolph, the Saxon missionary who died in AD 680, is thought to have visited 'Cnotta's Clearing' around the middle of the seventh century and established the first Christian church.

Children at Ropewalk school in the 1930s. The school was erected in 1842, mainly by subscription. A mixed and infants school, the average attendance in 1905 was 323 children. The master in 1905 was Mark Hill with his wife, Mrs M. Hill, being listed as mistress.

Ropewalk school in the 1930s. From right to left, back row: D. Smith, B. Knapton, M. Smith, J. Murgatroyd, E. Smith, I. Ramskill, A. Fish, -?-, H. Bailey, C. Tramner, C. Chesney, -?-. Second row from back: H. Robert, G. Wilson, M. Berry, M. Benson, J. Bridgeland, R. Downs, J. Simpson. Third row from back: D. Allsop, J. Ward, -?-, M. Lee, -?-, D. Thornton, I. Hart, P. Wright, -?-, M. Cockcroft, -?-, M. Hurst. Front: D. Woodall, A. Clayburn, R. Wood, K. Smith, R. Ward, D. Hayes, -?-, -?-, H. Daw.

Weeland Road School, which opened in 1893. It was erected in 1893 as a mixed school for 318 children, although the average attendance was 210. The schoolmaster in 1905 was William Salmon. The building on the right on the right is the police station, which is still in use, the school itself has been demolished.

Knottingley Bandstand, at Greenhouse playing fields. Knottingley Silver Prize Band display their trophies and perform for local school children at the coronation celebrations in 1953. The bandstand has since been demolished.

An early photograph showing the roundabout on the old A1. Oxley's garage was on the corner, the approach to Knottingley was from the bottom right, straight ahead to Pontefract, with traffic turning right to Ferrybridge and left to Doncaster.

Town Hall, Knottingley.

Knottingley Town Hall in the 1950s after the camber of the road was altered. During the blackout in the Second World War a bus carrying servicemen ploughed into the wall of the town hall with great loss of life. After the war, around 1946, the camber of the road was altered to prevent this happening again.

Knottingley Town Hall, early 1900s. The town hall was built in 1865. Tomlinson's shop is on the right and at this time there was no road into Ropewalk, only a footpath. The town hall remained the council offices until the 1950s and is still in use for functions today. In 1892 it contained a Mechanic's Institute, lecture rooms and classrooms, and reading rooms which were well provided with London newspapers.

The town hall corner in 1919, with the jubilee lamp-post in the middle of the road. Queen Victoria celebrated her Golden Jubilee in 1887 and her Diamond Jubilee in 1897. The war memorial was not built until 1921.

Knottingley War Memorial with St Botolph's in the background. According to the 'order of service' the memorial is described thus: 'It consists of a tall column of cornish grey granite, set upon a massive base, on which is inscribed the names of the fallen. A symbolical figure in bronze representing the Angel of Peace, surmounts the whole. The Angel with outspread wings holds in one hand the Trumpet heralding Peace and in the other the Wreath of victory. The site is enclosed by an ornamental semi-circular wall in Ackworth stone, with pillars and recesses at intervals. The Inscription on the Pedestal of the Monument is as follows: In glorious and everlasting memory of the men of Knottingley who died in the Great War, 1914-1918.'

A huge crowd attends the ceremony dedicating the war memorial on Sunday 25 September 1921. Colonel C.C. Moxon CMG, DSO unveiled the memorial and Revd F.E. Egerton, Revd W. Salisury and Revd H. Snowdon conducted the ceremony.

Two

Aire Street and Chapel Street

Aire Street in 1846, showing the bustling river and shopping trade. An association known as the Fishers' and Mariners' Society was situated in the premises of William Simpson Hepworth during the early part of the nineteenth century. Until 1936 the Shipwrecked Fishermen and Mariners' Society was still using the same premises, with T.M. Hepworth involved – this could have been the same society.

The top of Aire Street, looking down from the corner of Chapel Street, *c.* 1930. On the left is George Baker, shoe repairer (with a cover over the window) and Sutcliffe, watch and clock maker. On the right is Mary Hardy's, pots, pans and crockery and Ibbotson's fish and chips.

Lower Aire Street, pre-1930. Strawfold Close cottages, which were demolished in the 1930s, are on the right. The first shop on the left belonged to Hannah Rhodes and the tall building further down was Harker's watchmakers.

Aire Street shops in the early 1900s. Bramham's toys and trinkets became Meadow Dairy. Bradburn's barber shop and Hobman's shoe shop are shown with Herbert Hobman, holding Glenn Hobman in his arms, standing outside.

Staff pose alongside their window display at the Meadow Dairy, possibly in the 1950s.

A group of men congregate under a lamp-post in Aire Street, illustrating the lack of employment during the depression in the 1930s.

Aire Street, looking up towards St Botolph's, c. 1950. On the left is the farm shop.

Shops in the middle of Aire Street, opposite the Flatts. Nothing now remains of these shops and the whole of Aire Street is unrecognizable, only the view to the church remains the same.

Aire Street in the 1950s, showing the shops opposite the Flatts. In 1837 Sarah Rainsforth's academy was situated in Aire Street together with a shoe and hosiery warehouse, a druggist and a colour dealer and a gardener.

Looking towards Marsh End, from the start of the Flatts. In 1892 two master mariners, Samuel Frank and George Mann resided at Marsh End.

Looking up Aire Street towards St Botolph's and Chapel Street. The old schoolhouse in Chapel Street was used until twelve years ago as the public library. It is now a listed building. Until recently it was used as a boxing club though it is presently unoccupied.

Oxley's draper shop, Aire Street,
c. 1925. Emily Horncastle (left)
and Renee Firth are standing
outside the door.

Annie Downes outside her shop.
Her window display has possibly
been designed to celebrate the
1951 Festival of Britain or the 1953
Coronation celebrations.

Chapel Street showing Miss Swann's and Jackie Pearson's sweet shop at the turn of the century. At the back of the sweet shop was a private school. Brown's pawn shop, with the blind down, is also shown.

The Old Parsonage in Chapel Street. In 1803 an Act was passed which made it possible for a mortgage loan to be made towards the building of a parsonage house, before this time the incumbent would have had to pay for the building himself. In 1810 the parsonage was erected by Revd John Bailey, with a grant from Queen Anne's Bounty of £400.

Three
Ferrybridge

Ferrybridge War Memorial, from a postcard of around 1950. Ferrybridge was an important posting town, being situated approximately half way between London and Edinburgh. Ferrybridge also had it's own customs house. Letters were dispatched by horse post to Pontefract at 1.30 p.m. and to Selby at 1 p.m., from Thomas Arnall's post office.

Looking up Doncaster Road from the Square. From 1660 Ferrybridge was a very important postal station with posts to and from the West Riding being sorted and distributed there.

An early view of Ferrybridge Square, c. 1900. A group of children gather around the jubilee lamp-post. The bridge is visible in the background.

Ferrybridge Square, featuring the B&S bus which used to pick up at the lamp-post in the centre. Postboys, drivers and guards lived around the square to be near the inns, which catered for the coaching trade. Ferrybridge and Wetherby postboys were noted for their red striped waistcoats.

Ferrybridge Square during a flood in the 1950s. Floods were regular events, occurring when river levels were high. In the background are the towers of Ferrybridge A Power Station.

Ferrybridge School and schoolhouse, *c.* 1905. Ferrybridge Infants was built later behind the schoolhouse.

Ferrybridge Junior School in the 1970s.

Ferrybridge School hockey team, *c.* 1920. From left to right, back row: H. Peaker, C. Hatfield, -?-, F. Whitfield, -?-, -?-. Front: M. Hodgson, M. Till, -?-, -?-, G. Goodair, A. Wood.

Ferrybridge football team, posing with their trophies. From left to right, back row: B. Evans, G. Evans, B. Piper, F. Smith, H. Addy, J. Grice, A. Vause, M. Wood, B. Hepworth, W. Whitwell, -?-, E. Pickering. Front: T. Smith, B. Hibbett, H. Whitwell, I. Glew, C. Whitwell.

St Andrew's church, Ferrybridge on its new site in the 1970s. The church was moved from its old site, stone by stone, in 1952. Repeated winter flooding made the church unusable for long periods in its original location, inspiring Revd C.H. Branch to have the church moved and rebuilt in its present location.

A ceremony at Ferrybridge War Memorial, possibly in the 1920s. The memorial was erected on a piece of land adjacent to Toll Bridge House.

An aerial view of the Greyhound pub with Three Horse Shoes opposite, prior to demolition. An original coaching inn, the Greyhound was a split site inn with its stabling and postboy's tap on the other side of the road.

Ferrybridge Square in the1950s. A trade directory for 1837 describes Ferrybridge as 'a small but handsome and well built town, on the south bank of the River Aire, and on the Great North road, two miles north east of Pontefract, fifteen miles from Leeds and Doncaster and one hundred and seventy seven miles from London'.

The Golden Lion pub as it stands today. The inn, between 1786 and 1840, dealt mainly with the broad-wheeled vehicles which carried poorer passengers and parcels along the Great North Road. The Golden Lion was described as 'a house that was much frequented by the heavy luggage waggons which were on the road'. It was also the shipping and receiving house for the goods that came up the river from Hull by boat.

The Swan Inn and Glasshouse Yard, opposite the Golden Lion in the early 1900s. The Yorkshire Bottling Company was established here. The horses for the Swan Inn had to be led across the bridge before and after each change. The inn was kept by the Hall family at first, then Samuel Thwaites was landlord in the latter days of the coaching era. When mails first began to be carried by coach in 1786 the whole length of the road, from Ferrybridge to Tadcaster, was worked by Mr Hall's father, Mr John Hall.

The Old Greyhound Inn. This is situated on the same site as that occupied by the present day pub. In 1800 the inn was run by Mary Moody, who was joined in partnership by her son-in-law Samuel Rusby in 1803.

The Three Horse Shoes pub was opposite the Greyhound. Harry Beach was the landlord for many years. Through a passage, to the rear of the pub were changing rooms that were used by Ferrybridge Amateurs Football Club.

Ferrybridge Pottery, possibly in the latter half of the nineteenth century. The works were established in 1792 by William Tomlinson, in partnership with Mr Seaton, Mr Foster, Mr T. Smith and Mr Thompson.

An early engraving of Ferrybridge, showing the river trade and coaches travelling across the bridge. Coaches to London in 1837 ran at 1.30 p.m., 6.15 p.m. and 10.30 p.m. They ran to York and the North at 5 a.m. and 6 a.m. At the largest coaching inn in Ferrybridge, the Angel which was kept by Dr Alderson, it was not uncommon to turn out fifty pairs of horses in one day. The Highflyer and the Leeds Union coaches were horsed from here and also the two Royal Mail coaches to Robin Hood's Well.

The launch of the Pomfret-Goole lifeboat at the side of the Golden Lion pub, by Lady Houghton in December 1865. The *Pontefract Advertiser*, dated 2 December 1865, stated that the boat, having had her harbour trial in the Regent Canal Dock, London would be exhibited next week before launching. The vessel was taken to Goole to be exhibited and then transported to its ultimate destination of Tynemouth. Richard Mockton Milnes, Lord Houghton of Fryston Hall is buried at the churchyard at the old site of St Andrews, Ferrybridge.

Workers and ware inside Ferrybridge Pottery. The manufactory was known as the Knottingley Pottery until 1804, when it was changed for the convenience of foreign correspondence as at that time Ferrybridge was a post town of significance.

Pottery ware from Ferrybridge. The marks used were 'TOMLINSON & CO' impressed on the bottom of the ware, 'WEDGWOOD & CO' during Ralph Wedgwood's connection with the firm and also 'FERRYBRIDGE', of which one variety has the 'D' reversed.

Traffic over the old bridge at Ferrybridge, possibly in the 1930s. The bridge was later closed and a new bridge for the A1 was constructed, luckily the old bridge remains in place although inaccessible to traffic.

Ferrybridge A Power Station under construction, on 7 May 1926. Pictured is the Eastern Elevation, which was the boiler house side, looking across the river from the Great North Road.

Ferrybridge Power Station after completion in 1927. The power station closed down in 1957. However, the main building is still intact and is used as an office and workshop.

Ferrybridge A Power Station. Ferrybridge B was commissioned in 1959 and is still in use today. It is a coal-fired plant and currently produces 282 MW of power per year.

Advertising material for Yorkshire Electric Power Company, celebrating the opening of Ferrybridge A Power Station.

Ferrybridge C Power Station collapsing on 6 September 1968. Ferrybridge C was commissioned in 1968 and is still in current use, it uses coal to produce 2000 MW of power per year.

Ferrybridge Lock, with Ferrybridge A in the background, *c.* 1950. The vessel *Reliance* is moored in the lock. The bridge shown was built by John Carr of York and was opened to travellers in June 1804. In stone panels, on opposite sides, inside parapets of the bridge are the names of John Carr (architect) and Bernard Hartley (builder) of Pontefract. Ferrybridge Lock was opened at 10 a.m. on 20 July 1826, after which 'the principal officers of the establishment, with their friends set forward to Goole in a fly-packet' where they arrived at about 3.30 p.m.

Four

Sporting

Knottingley Town cricket team. From left to right, back row: Gordon Wiltshire, Ken Gray, Albert Perry, Fred Starks, David Hurst, Malcolm Matthewman. Front row: Eric Slater, Ronnie Walker, Fred Sidwell, Reg Link, Grant Talbot.

Knottingley Cricket Club, in 1911. Pictured from left to right, back row are: J. Day, J. White, G. Beaumont, W. Metcalfe, J. Ingle, P. Brears, J. Cawthorne. Centre: H. Spink, T. Poulson, A. Link, A. Billbrough, H. Bentley, G. France. Reclining at the front are P. Thompson and J. Brook.

Knottingley cricket team with trophy, c. 1930. From left to right, among those on the back row: Jack Talbot, Frank Arnold, ? Barton, John Sykes, Horace Whitwell (umpire), Bill Hepworth. Centre: Billy Whitehead (?), Fred France, Granville Bagley, ? Worfolk, Harold Cooper. Front row: Walt Whitwell, Charlie Blackburn .

Knottingley Adults Amateur Football Club, 1909. The only players which have been identified are a few on the centre row: Lawrence Aaron (second from the left), Percy Turpin (fourth from the left) and one of the Branford family (sixth from the left).

Knottingley Rovers Amateur Football Club, 1913/14. From left to right, back row: ? Hanson, Ronald Brooks (?), -?-, Len Wrightson, -?-. Centre: Bob Dawson, Percy Davies, -?-, Bob Drinkwater. Front: George Davies, Fred Hart, ? Kelly, Charlie Adamson (a teacher at the church school), -?-.

Gregg's glassworks team, with the Aire trophy that they won in an inter-works competition. From left to right, back row: Jack Knight, Walter Oldfield, Harold Appleyard, Harry Dobson, Tom Davies, Ernie Tunningley, Frank Slater, Charley Spence. Front row: Mick Tunningley, Terry Davies, Bunny Turner, Jimmy Smith, Charlie Temple.

Bagley's football team, 1951/52. From left to right, back row: Derek Eades, Tommy Hirst, Eric Rhodes, George Kemp, Jack Knight, John Pickersgill, Mil Bedworth (senior). Centre: Mil Bedworth (junior), Harry Downes, Harry Dobson, Les Johnson, Charlie Temple. Front: Colin Wallis, Arthur Johnson.

Bagley's Recs rugby team, in the cricket field in the 1930s. From left to right, back row: Joe Gawthorpe, Jim Taylor, Albert Burden, Noel Swales, Charlie Wilson, Henry Adams. Centre: Blant Taylor, George Lightfoot, Bill Skelton, Arthur Johnson, A. Walker. Front row: Shimmnert Baxter, Albert Bagley, Eric Collings, Mil Bedworth.

Bagley's Recs team in Sleepy Valley during the 1940s. From left to right, back row: -?-, Ernie Taylor, George Briars, Tunny Gates, ? Hancock, Dennis Hargrave, Jack Sunderland, Eddie Perfect, George Bagley, Harry Hargraves. Front row: Jack Briars, Lawrence Askin, Ramsey Ashton, Don Martindale, -?-, Jackie Fennell, -?-.

Knottingley Flyers rugby team outside Beehive, *c.* 1920. From left to right, back row: -?-, Harry Heath, Frank Burden, -?-, George Knapton, -?-, Jimmy Lowther, Harry Savage, -?-, -?-, Tommy Moon. Centre: Henry Adams, Noel Swales, Blant Taylor, Bill Skelton, Cliff Lloyd, -?-, -?-. Front row: Mick Lloyd, ? Swales (?), Albert Bagley.

Knottingley Rovers rugby team, *c.* 1930.

School football team, 1927/28. From left to right, back row: Mr Tomlinson, Arnold Watmough, Jimmy Moon, Roland Fox, Reg Kelly, Major Harker, Percy Rhodes, Mr Threadgold. Front row: Charlie Fieldhouse, Ralph Cawthorn, Fred Cowling (captain), Dick Hutchinson, Gordon Addy.

Englands Lane School football team of 1960. Tony Morrell and Dave Hookham (teachers) are on the left and right respectively. From left to right, back row: Stephen Sheard, Barry Hinchcliffe, John Hargraves, Keith Tomlinson, Derek England, John Dixon, Phil Sutton. Front row: Stephen Guy, Graham Haslam, Robert Bedford, Colin Brown, Neil Hutchinson, Roy Scaife.

Weeland Road School football team, 1920/21. From left to right, back row: J. Morris, H. Burdin, T. Masterton, O. Adamson, P. Wilson, B. Glendenning, W. Hollingworth. Centre: E. Lewis, T. Rhodes, H. Townend, H. Downey. Front row: A. Shaw, H. Whitwell, F. Gordon.

National School football team, 1921. From left to right, back row: Henry Rhodes, George Miller, Alf Skelton. Centre: Jack Tether, Ned Shaw, Dick Hughes, George Burton. Front row: Ernest Turner, George Halcrow, Ted Stones, George Elsley, Billy Addy.

Ferrybridge school football team. Left to right, back row: Dave Owen, Dick Preston, Horace Wright, Frank Smith, Albert Vause, ? Blewitt, George Preston. Front row: Clarence Boggett, Lionel King, -?-, Sonny Hadfield, -?-.

Junior XI football team, 1956/57. From left to right, back row: Keith Tunningley, Arthur Ridge, Eric Schofield, Derek Emmerson, Roy Horton. Centre: -?-, Bobby Haigh, -?-, -?-, Barry Pickersgill. Front row: Harold Foster, Ernie Brown, Peter Hinchcliffe.

Ferrybridge Amateur Football Club. From left to right, back row: Ben Gates, -?-, Ralph Cawthorn, -?-, Fred Sidwell, Bert Cook. Front row: Lou Pearson, Roy Milner, Jimmy Swales, Charlie Harrison, -?-.

Ferrybridge Amateur Football Club. From left to right, back row: -?-, Joey Smithey, Wally Brown, Fred Sidwell, -?-, Ralph Cawthorn, Bert Cotterill, Ernie Richardson, Ben Gates. Front row: Lou Pearson, -?-, Charlie Harrison, John Swales, Bert Cook.

Ropewalk School, KCSS first VII netball team, 1956/57. From left to right, back row: Dora King, -?-, Jean Finney. Front row: ? Smith, -?-, Mrs Wordsworth, Joan Holland, Ann Tomlinson.

KCSS senior VII netball team, 1956/57. From left to right, back row: ? Smith, -?-, Jean Finney. Front row: Dora King, -?-, Mrs Wordsworth, Joan Holland, Ann Tomlinson.

The All England Angling Champions with their trophy in the 1920s. Standing at the back, are Harry Mason (left) and Austwick Dobson. Front, from left to right are: Harry Sweeting, Percy Davies, Lawrence Aaron, Jim Durnow.

Les Bell (bottom) with Arthur Ridge (top) wrestling in 1951 at the Festival of Britain celebrations. After the austerity of the war years this was a wonderful way to celebrate the new decade.

Five

Industry

Knottingley Canal, c. 1950. A barge with 'Tom Puddings' is shown navigating the waterway.
These were introduced by W.H. Bartholomew as a 'compartment boat train', as he called them
in his 1862 patent application.

Carter's Brewery, which according to the 1881 census employed approximately forty men and a clerk. In 1891 the Knottingley Brewery Co. produced ale, porter and Indian bitter beer. They were also wine and spirit merchants and cigar importers.

Bagley's glassworks in the Bendles, in the 1950s. Flyboats and steam packets picked up passengers for Goole and Hull here. In 1837 the steam packet, *Magnet*, travelled to Goole daily at 6.30 a.m., after the arrival of coaches from Leeds, Wakefield and other towns. The steam packet would return according to the tide.

Knottingley gasworks, with a group of workers in 1905. Kelly's directory of 1892 states that 'the town is lighted with gas from works belonging to a company'. Thomas Speak was listed as the secretary and Thomas Worfolk as the manager.

The railway sidings at Ferrybridge A Power Station on 7 May 1926, during the general strike. The strike was undertaken in support of the miners who were resisting the imposition of lower pay and longer hours. The strike was frustrated by the use of troops to maintain essential services and in the end lasted only nine days.

Workmen in the Lime Quarry. In 1861 thirteen firms were working in lime production, but by 1927 no firms were producing this commodity in the area. Lime was used mainly in agriculture and road building, it was transported as a second cargo on the canals, with the boats arriving laden with coal and departing laden with limestone. It was only excavated to a depth of seven yards, as the water table below made any deeper excavation much more costly.

A group of workers from the glassworks prepare for an outing in the early 1900s. Burdin's Glass Company was formed in 1887 and mainly produced carboys to contain acid, and small flint bottles.

The water tower at Knottingley, c. 1905.

Workers at Kings Mills, probably in the 1920s. Immediately downstream from the mill the company had a dry dock and yard. In 1902 the plant was renovated and the mill was leased to Ellis Williamson for £410 per annum. A large steam engine and a Lancashire boiler were installed in 1903.

The fire at Sun Flour Mills in November 1963. Police and fire crews had to sift through the rubble after the fire had been put out. In 1962 the mill became part of Garfield Weston's Allied Mills group, which supplied flour to the major biscuit and cake manufacturers in the north of England.

Warren Mill, built c. 1814 and first leased in 1815. Mr Chadwick who leased the mill asked for a reduction in rent in 1830 but then went into receivership. The mill was then re-let to Mr Jackson, for 300 guineas per annum.

The old water wheel at Knottingley Mill. In 1848, after one of the sails of the mill was smashed in a gale, William Jackson who leased the mill erected a water wheel in the vacant race of the water mill and harnessed it to the windmill's machinery.

Packing glass at Jackson's Glass Co. Bagley's glassworks was taken over by Jackson's Glass Company who then became part of the Rockware group.

The medallion awarded to Bagley Wild Co. at the Paris Exhibition of 1878. The company was founded in 1871 as a bottle works, however after financial difficulties it was dissolved and in 1898 a private company was formed under the name of Bagley and Company. In 1912 they diversified into the new areas of lead crystal manufacture and pressed glass making, as well as bottle manufacturing.

A trade stand of Bagley Crystal Glass Co. In 1924 the firm exhibited at the Wembley exhibition and Queen Mary purchased some pieces of glassware. Later the design was marketed as the 'Queen's Choice'. In 1934 Queen Mary further purchased some of the new coloured glassware.

The face of the Paris Medallion. The first of the great international exhibitions was held at Crystal Palace in 1851. Between 1851 and 1970 around thiry-four major exhibitions were held around the world. In 1928 a convention was signed by thirty-five countries to govern the frequency and methods of organization.

A trade catalogue. Lead crystal was only produced for two years, pressed glass however was in production until 1975 and was sold as crystal glassware. Initially production was limited to clear glass in everyday items e.g. glasses, bowls and clear table sets.

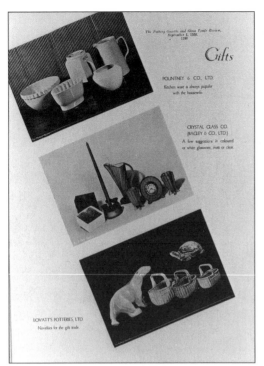

A trade catalogue showing crystal glassware. During the early 1930s coloured glass was introduced under the name of 'Crystaltynt', this was available in the colours of green, blue, pink and amber.

Mr James Betchetti, blowing bottles at Burdin's glassworks. Air was blown through the hollow rod to make a bubble shape, this was then carried away and a smear of water was added to make the glass at the neck brittle and the rod was removed. The bottle was then lifted with a 'puntil' and the neck and the ring were added and smoothed. The finished bottle was then placed in a kiln for annealing and finally it would be left to cool for forty-eight hours.

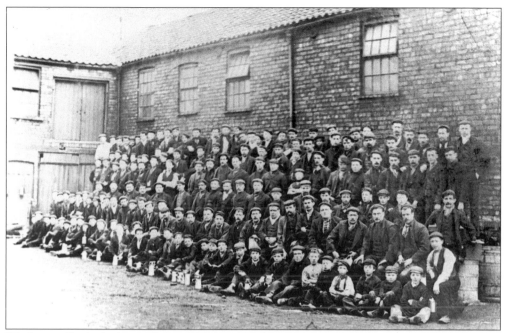

Workers at Bagley's glassworks, c. 1906. In 1906 the 160 strong work force was exclusively male but by the time of the royal visit a mixed workforce of 800 was employed.

Preparing for the royal visit to Bagley's in 1937. During World War Two the main production at Bagley's was beer glasses to be supplied to the NAAFI, although it was hard to keep up with the breakages! The machinery was also used to turn shell cases and battery containers for the RAF.

Making pressed glassware in 1937. During this process a gather of glass is dropped into a mould and a plunger then squeezes the glass between itself and the outer mould which then forms the final shape. Both the mould and the plunger may be patterned to impart decorative designs to the object being made.

A reproduction of the first bottle making machine. Around 1866 Ferrybridge postmaster Mr Joshua Arnall thought of a way of mechanically blowing bottles. The technique he thought up was then modified by the manager of the Ferrybridge foundry, Mr H.M. Ashley. In 1866 the Ashley-Arnall Company was formed and a patent was applied for on the machine.

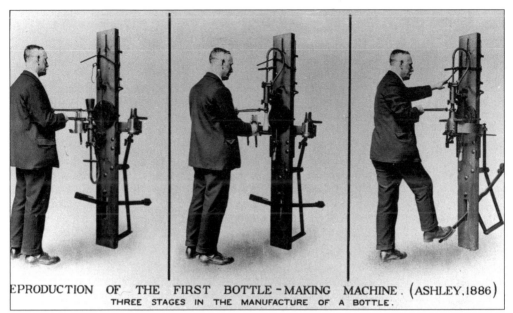

EPRODUCTION OF THE FIRST BOTTLE-MAKING MACHINE. (ASHLEY,1886)
THREE STAGES IN THE MANUFACTURE OF A BOTTLE.

First bottle making machine in use. By 1892, 2,160 bottles a day could be turned out by the machine with more uniformity than hand-blown glass, and at considerably less expense. In 1899 William Bagley bought the patent of the machine for his company, which affected the production of other local firms who did not have similar equipment and who were unable to compete.

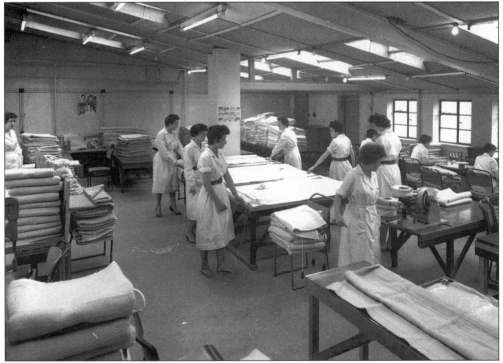

Warmabed electric blanket manufacturer, possibly in the 1940s or '50s. The firm still manufactures and services electric blankets today.

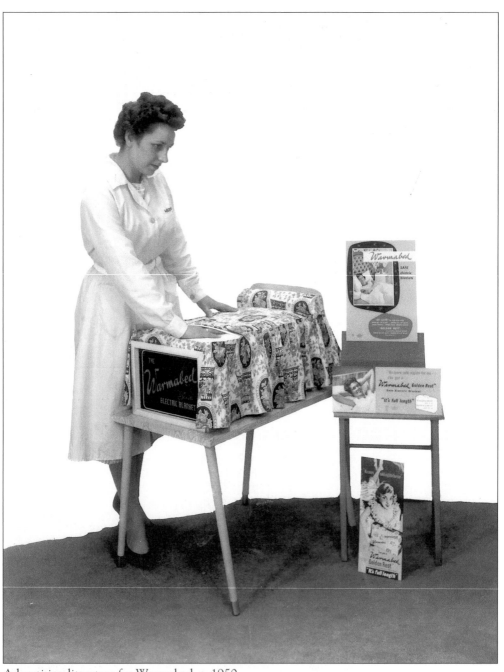

Advertising literature for Warmabed, *c*. 1950.

Inside Knottingley Brewery in the 1870s. It is possibly Charles Dawrant the engine tenter who is pictured. At the time of the 1871 census Mr Dawrant was thirty-three and was resident with his wife and five children, aged between six months and eleven years, in Knottingley.

Heating rivets at Harker's shipyard. Riveters were skilled men who were employed in gangs of three or four. The rivets, which were bolts of about three inches long were placed on a metal grille, with the head uppermost, and then placed in a coke fired portable brazier. A labourer, using long handled tongs would then position the rivet through holes drilled in the metal plates of the vessel. Using a 'gun' worked by compressed air the riveter would then burr over the end of the bolt shaft, while at the other side of the plate the rivet was held in position by another colleague.

Workers at the tar distillery. Yorkshire Tar Distillers Ltd was formed in 1926, although a business known as the Aire Tar Company was founded much earlier – in 1877 – near Bank Dole Lock between Weeland Road and the Selby junction of the Aire and Calder Canal.

Six

Shipping

Harker's workforce with the *Constance H*, which was built in 1930. The *Constance H* was launched on 17 September 1930.

Harker's shipyard in the 1950s. In 1918 the business, which had been purchased by Mark Stainsby and John George Lyon in 1877, was registered as John Harker Ltd and at this time consisted of seven dumb barges drawn by steam tugs. James William Kipping, John Harker's son-in-law, was retained as manager.

William Kipping, built at Harker's, was the first vessel launched in August 1929. The *William Kipping* was a 150 ton barge which was launched stern first – a risky operation if the water level was too high as the stern would be forced upwards.

An early view of Bank Dole Reach with the chimneys of the chemical works in the background, and a large amount of vessels moored. On the bank in front of the chimneys are large stacks of barrels.

Bank Dole Lock, which connects the canal and the river. The Aire and Calder Navigation Act was passed by Parliament on 3 April 1699, and was the first navigation scheme to be undertaken by an Act of Parliament – preceding any other scheme by fifty years. The Act, which was passed, allowed 'cuts' to be dug to bypass hazards, thereby saving time and mileage. The slopes of the Aire were trimmed to prevent silting and flooding, and locks and pounds were to be built to bypass mill weirs.

Launch of the *Josephine* on 17 January 1942. In the background are launches which were built for the RAF during the war to refuel seaplanes. The *Josephine* was a coal dumb barge which was built for Hargreaves, Leeds.

The *Empire Rancher*, built in 1942. The Ministry of War Transport used it to transport coal, from South Wales to Gloucester Power Station. In the same year Harker's purchased the area of land which had previously comprised three separate shipyards in order to expand their yard.

A Caulker at work on a vessel in Harker's shipyard, pre-1960. Special tools with a chisel end were used to burr over the end of the overlapping metal plates to produce a smooth waterproof surface for the ship.

An inshore trawler, built by Harker's for Jenkinson & Co. of Scarborough. The vessel was launched on 8 June 1967. By the 1960s Harker's had diversified from producing mainly barges to building other types of craft as well.

The *Rebus Stone* moored in 1963. Built for Cory Tank Lighterage Ltd, London she was launched 17 January 1963.

Aerial views of Harker's shipyard. A major reconstruction of the yard took place in the late 1950s, however in the 1960s the carrying trade began to decline and so the company diversified into the building of pleasure craft and trawlers, although they did continue with their repair work on barges.

The *Beldale*, grounded at Knottingley. This was a launch which didn't quite go according to plan – showing that despite meticulous planning, things could and did go wrong on occasion!

Launch of the *Southdale* illustrating the scale of the ships. Around 1936 the policy of naming boats after Yorkshire dales was introduced and at this time the vessels began to feature the Harker house flag on their funnels.

Teesdale H, launched in June 1951 by Lady Wingate Saul. The crew's quarters were surprisingly comfortable, having bunk beds, a washroom, toilet and a galley complete with an electric oven – this was in accordance with the council certificate which registered the vessel as a dwelling.

The Point End slipway at Harker's shipyard was built in 1947 for survey and repair work and was modified in 1950s. The new slipway enabled two large vessels lying parallel to each other to be raised sideways from the water for servicing. In 1947 the custom of raising the house flag above the offices during a launch was introduced.

John Branford, a shipbuilder, was born in Knottingley in 1838. His first vessel was constructed from salvaged timber, and he regularly bought second-hand timber from auctions held in Wakefield. In the 1881 census he was also listed as being a grocer and corn dealer at Racca Green.

The first screw steamer, *Message*, which was built by John Branford in 1893. At 100 feet in length it was so long that people wishing to enter the Commercial Inn had to crawl under the vessel to enter the inn. Newspaper reports of the time carried the ship's name as the *Messenger* although the shipping records list the vessel as the *Message*.

A keel in full sail on the canal in the 1890s. The design and rig of these vessels has hardly changed from Tudor times, and it is possible that they were derived from Viking ships. Even the name dates back to the Saxon word for a longship, which was a 'coel'.

Knottingley canal, *c.* 1950 showing water transportation. 'Tom Puddings' were first used in 1865, they are still used at Knottingley for short haul coal carrying to Ferrybridge Power Station. They earned their name due to their lilting gait.

The *Martindale H*, pictured in the Bendles in the 1950s. The Wesleyan chapel is in the background. Being craft of between 100 and 800 tons carrying capacity, many of the dales barges were too large to be used on local waterways, although they were the pride of the Harker fleet.

Seven

Transport

A goods train travels through Knottingley Station. The station once had five platforms with a covered roof. In its heyday Knottingley was a changing point for passengers using the Wakefield to Goole trains and the trains from Leeds to Doncaster, it was consequently an extremely busy station.

The Coronation bus with its crew in 1953. The destination on the front of the bus reads 'Peace via Prosperity', with the very patriotic slogan 'Elizabeth II, Long May She Reign' written along the side of the vehicle.

A lorry delivering Jackson's glass. Jackson's Glass Company was the firm which took over Bagley's Glass Company.

One of Warmabed's publicity vans. The firm manufactured and serviced electric blankets and is still in operation today.

Glass was originally transported in hand-made wicker baskets. Two sizes of basket had to be made, one to transport glass and the other to be used for pottery. Mr Pickard was the local carrier at the turn of the century. In Kelly's directory for 1892 Thomas Birdsall of Aire Street is listed as a basket maker.

Mr Pickard and his donkey preparing to transport glass bottles, c. 1900. The instability of the load must have been extreme, requiring very careful packing.

The Ferry Boat at Aire Street, Knottingley, *c.* 1905. The ferryboat allowed the people of Knottingley access to Brotherton marsh for a fare of 1d.

The ferry, *Duchess of Leeds*, being dismantled on the bank on the left hand side. These traditional vessels were built with the planks forming the hull being flush at the edges, rather than overlapping.

A goods train on the Doncaster branch line behind Elmhurst Grove. Jackson's glassworks and the houses at Hillgarth are in the background.

Knottingley Station and goods yard, looking from Headlands Lane with the signal box on the right and an engine shed on the left. In 1871 the railway station was listed as a residence with the stationmaster William Essame, his wife and six children living there. Three porters and an inspector along with their families were also listed as residents.

A group of railway workers who worked at the 'pickling tank', prior to 1930. Railway sleepers were treated here. Lying down on the left is George Tunningley.

Arthur Suggett was stationmaster at Knottingley in December 1955.

Knottingley Boys Brigade get ready to leave for camp on Knottingley Station, possibly in the 1960s. They were a large troop and often camped at Whitby and Scarborough. Their band led many local parades.

This was probably Sam Maeer's first lorry, outside Bramley's shop in the Holes, c. 1920. As can be seen the lorry had solid tyres, and an admiring crowd!

Knottingley firefighters in 1946 with the fire engine, which hooked on the back of a car. From left to right: Bill Middleton, Albert Hague, William Askin, Albert Murgatroyd, -?-, Alfie Parker, B. Birkett.

Knottingley firefighters at the Festival of Britain in 1951. By this time they had a full size engine. Left to right, back row: Charlie Askin, Albert Taylor, John Rhodes, Fred Smith, Ted Kellyn, Bill Birkett. Front row: George Reynolds, Alf Murgatroyd, Tommy Garner, Jimmy Smith.

Mr Poskitt of Beal poses alongside his lorry.

One of Bagley's horses prepares for Howden Show. Fred Furniss is pictured with 'Phyllis'. During their working day the horses were used to haul the trucks around the yard.

Eight

Buildings

The Duke of York pub, which was situated in the Holes. In 1837 William Smithson, who was also a brick and tile maker and iron founder at Selby, was the landlord. The pub closed in 1968.

Sculpture House and the White Swan Inn in the early 1900s. The sign on the pub is the Royal Antaveludian Order of Buffaloes. The building on the extreme right is Leeman's saddler's shop.

The Midland Bank building prior to its demolition. In 1892 banking services in Knottingley could be found at the town hall, which accommodated Leatham, Tew & Co., who drew on Barkley, Bevan & Co. of London or in the National School Room, where the Yorkshire Penny Bank, which was open on Monday between 6 and 7 p.m., was situated.

Detail of the sculptured fireplace in Sculpture House. Originally this was part of the Manor House of the Ingram family. The fireplace was described as a 'most exquisite and antique piece of sculpture in stone' according to Forrest's *History of Knottingley*.

An early view of Sculpture House, *c.* 1900. The building was formerly the western section of the Ingram's Manor House. The west wing itself was demolished and the east wing became the Swan Inn.

The Anvil Inn, *c.* 1930. Jimmy Green, who was the landlord from 1928 to 1933, is standing outside. In 1892 the landlord was William Birkitt and the inn was situated in Banks Lane.

The Bay Horse Inn at Hill Top. The inn was in existence as far back as 1837 when the landlord was William Taylor, by 1892 the landlord was Joe Beaumont.

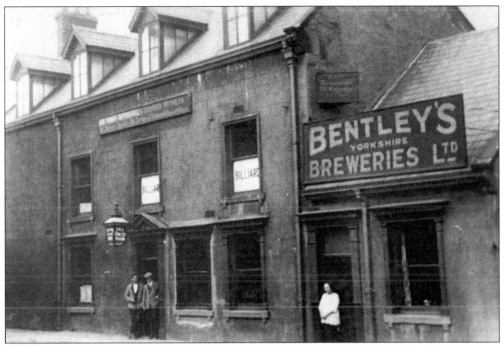

The Sailor's Home, Chapel Street, *c.* 1925. John Heptinstall was the landlord between 1924 and 1929. The landlord in 1892 was Charles Knapton.

A later view of the Sailor's Home, which was previously named the Wheatsheaf and was known locally as 'the Corner'.

The Lamb Inn situated in Weeland Road, c. 1905. Many Knottingley families were in the horse hauling business and it was common practice to stable their horses at local inns. The Lamb Inn began life as a 'pot shop' or 'beer house', but in 1904 it was granted a licence that was transferred from the Anchor pub. In recent years, the pub has been replaced by the present building, which stands on the opposite side of Weeland Road.

The Waggon and Horses, Aire Street. George Spence was the landlord in 1837 and Joe Wrigley was the landlord between 1904 and 1908.

The Waggon and Horses on Aire Street after renovation. In Kelly's directory of 1892 Henry Shay is listed as the landlord.

St Botolph's church before the addition of the tower in 1873. Originally a Chapel of Ease to Pontefract church, it was made a perpetual curacy in 1725. The first incumbent was Frances Lascelles, who was appointed in 1717 under the benefice of the Ingram family, who were the Lords of the Manor.

An interior view of St Botolph's in the 1870s, before alterations were made. The church was thoroughly remodelled in 1888 when a new chancel was built, the nave reseated and the galleries taken down at a total cost of over £2,000.

A later view of St Botolph's, *c.* 1900, after the addition of the tower.

An interior view, after the alterations had taken place. The chancel fittings were donated by Mr G.W. Carter of Lime Grove, who also presented the stained-glass east window.

St Botolph's before alteration, showing the box pews and gallery. In 1872 Ebenezer Rushton Talbot became parish priest. He considered that the 'private pew system is a hindrance, for too many parishioners are excluded by private pews'.

After alteration in the 1880s the pews became open and the gallery was removed. Mrs Rhodes (née Moorhouse) of New Zealand provided the pulpit, font and lectern as a memorial for her family.

A memorial window in St Botolph's church. William Jackson, the miller, was churchwarden at St Botolph's until his death in 1873. His family erected a window to his memory in the church.

St Botolph's Mother's Union, c. 1920. At the front left are Mrs Rhodes with son Alan, front right are Mrs Hoole and daughter Catherine. Included on the front row are: Mrs Coates (fourth from the left), Revd Egerton (fifth left), Mrs Petty (sixth left), Mrs Stanhope (seventh left), Mrs Lawson (eighth left). Included on the middle row are: A. Clayburn (second left), Mrs Cooper (third left), Mrs Reynolds (eleventh left).

Christ Church, *c.* 1950. William Moorhouse of Marine Villa obtained a grant to build a new church in Knottingley in 1848. The church was built to accommodate 570 people and the pews were rent free. The Incorporated Society for the enlargement, building and repair of churches provided the money.

Christ Church was consecrated on Wednesday 12 October 1848, by Archbishop Vernon Harcourt of York. The first services were conducted by the Bishop of Madras, Thomas Dealtry, a former Knottingley man. The first incumbent at the church was Thomas Davy who was instituted in June 1848 and who remained at the church until 1871. Horace Wood replaced Davy and by 1877 he reported that he was preaching three sermons every weekend – although the morning attendance was poor the evening attendance was about 180 people. The Sunday school was very active, with 100 children. In addition a weekly bible-reading study group was formed.

The interior of Christ Church, Knottingley, which was demolished in 1968. In 1890 a stained-glass east window was erected by Mrs Rhodes as a memorial to her father, Mr William Moorhouse. Christ Church was described in 1892 as 'a building of stone in the Decorated style, consisting of chancel, nave, transepts, north porch, vestry and a belfry containing three bells'.

The Wesleyan chapel (with its clock) and the schoolroom, which is now the chapel, situated next to it. The Wesleyans first came to Knottingley in 1784, in the early years there were only 4 members, however within 50 years the group had grown in number to 254. The new Wesleyan chapel was dedicated on 11 June 1846.

The organ and gallery, inside the Wesleyan chapel. Sometime before 1900 the original pews and pulpit were removed and replaced by the present ones. In 1907 a schoolhouse was added on land next to the chapel.

The L&YR Hotel shown in it's heyday, *c.* 1930. It was named after the local line, the Lancashire & Yorkshire Railway, which was established in 1846-47.

The L&YR Hotel station approach, prior to its closure in 1966 and subsequent demolition. The hotel is listed in a trade directory of 1892 with George Simpson named as landlord.

Lime Grove, the home of the Carter family, pictured in the late 1880s. According to the census return of 1881 the head of the family was George William Carter who was married to Elizabeth McMaster Carter who was born in Ireland. George Carter was a barrister although he was not in practice. He was however an active partner in Carter's brewery

The drawing room in Lime Grove in the 1880s. In 1881 only three servants were listed as living in the house, one of whom was the children's nurse, the other a cook and the third a housemaid. Daily help of course was not listed, but must have been used – the amount of work required for the upkeep of the house must have been enormous.

The Carter children, and their governess, Nurse Nixon, are pictured in the gardens at Lime Grove in the late 1880s.

The wonderful Victorian nursery of the Carter children, showing a variety of toys. The comparison between the poverty of most of the children in the area and the privileged lifestyle of the Carter children is amply illustrated here.

The dining room at Lime Grove in the 1880s. The key to the decoration of this room was obviously in the placing of their possessions – the many paintings and ornaments. A great status symbol, the profusion of fine possessions would have indicated to anyone entering the house how successful the owner was.

The conservatory at Lime Grove in the 1880s. As no gardener is listed in the 1881 census then it must be assumed that a jobbing gardener came in daily to do the work. In the 1892 trade directory two jobbing gardeners were listed, David Heald and Thomas Lawson.

Nine

Dakky's

Knottingley's first Carnival Queen, Miss Doris Ellerington, is pictured with her attendants in 1932. The pictures in this section were all taken by a travelling photographer known as Dakky, who set up his studio in a hut at the side of the canal. The photographs were developed and captioned by him and then sold as postcards. All of the photographs shown were taken during the 1930s.

'Happy Days'. From left to right: Mr Vause, Cliff Blissett, Edwin Thornton, 'Muckboat' Johnson, -?-, -?-, Mr Norton.

Christ Church Brownies, outside Jones' fish shop, Low End Knottingley, in 1939. From left to right, back row: Betty Garbutt, Eileen Holmes, Joyce Murgatroyd, Olive Mowbray, Margaret Reynolds, Irene Ramskill, Lilian O'Driscoll, Mary Meakin, Alma Thompson, Miss Ellis. Front row: Sarah Rothery, Doreen Eskriett, Ursula Backhouse, Mildred Stones, Joyce Lightowler, Joyce Darley, Daisy Hopkinson.

Knottingley Carnival Queen of 1936, Mary Middleton, is pictured with her attendant.

Carnival revellers along the parade route in 1936, possibly outside the Carnival Queen's house.

A group of people are pictured along the carnival route, in 1936.

George Jackson's milk cart in the 1930s. Pictured from left to right are George Lightowler, George Jackson and Harry Jackson.

Children wait impatiently along the route for the carnival procession to appear in 1936.

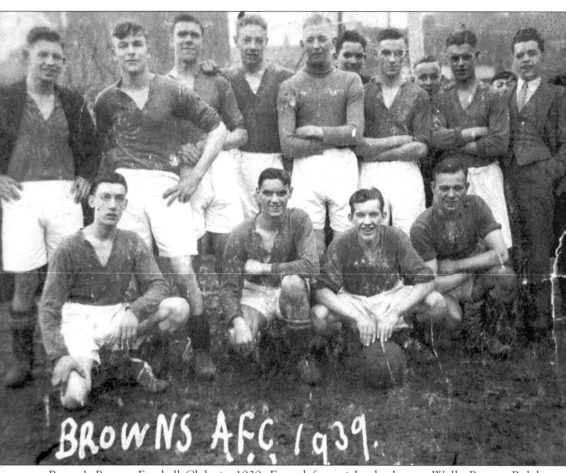

Brown's Pottery Football Club, in 1939. From left to right, back row: Wally Brown, Ralph Dawson, Harry Dobson, George Asquith, Ben Taylor, Eddie Lund, Fred Johnson, Ken Draper, Ben Bolland. Front row: Billy Wagstaff, Sam Whitfield, George Bolland, -?-.

Ten
Celebrations

Knottingley Town Hall, in 1951. It was illuminated courtesy of YEB for the Festival of Britain, they also paid for the illumination of St Botolph's church. On 2 May 1951 the King opened the Festival of Britain from the steps of St Paul's Cathedral.

Miss Harriet Stephenson launches *Tynedale H*, one of the Dales series of barges built by Harker's shipyard. The vessel later operated in the Tyne Tees area.

The 'Captain', one of Bagley's glasswork's horses, with Charlie Sheard, prepares for a show at Howden.

The royal visit to Bagley's glassworks on 21 October 1937. King George VI, Queen Elizabeth and the Princess Royal were shown around the works. The Queen was presented with a Marine Bowl, which was a low circular bowl moulded with fishes and crabs. A special commemorative plate of pressed glass was produced which was presented to employees of the firm and Knottingley schoolchildren. This plate was later remoulded to commemorate a royal visit to Canada, and was sold there in great numbers.

The Investiture of Councillor George Fozzard JP, 8 December 1954. From left to right are George Fozzard, Revd Beaumont and Sir Thomas Tomlinson BEM. The shield on the wall is the Knottingley coat of arms. An appeal was held to provide money to buy the chain, which was invested by County Alderman Sir Thomas Tomlinson BEM, and dedicated by Revd Beaumont. After the ceremony the guests were invited to a dinner held at the Winston Hotel, Womersley Road, Knottingley. The menu comprised grapefruit juice, cream of chicken or tomato soup, halibut and cream sauce, roast chicken with potatoes, brussels sprouts and marrowfat peas. To follow was apple or mince tart and cream with cheese and biscuits and finally coffee.

The church school percussion group rehearse for Pontefract Music Festival in 1936. Their rehearsals obviously paid dividends as they won a prize. Jimmy Spence is conducting. From left to right, back row: Philip Backhouse, Jackie Blanchard, George Banks, Harry Downes, Gordon Adams, John Steel, Jack Hall. Centre: Hilda Thompson, Derek Hardisty, Doreen Peel, Ronnie Hargraves, Rosa Sheard, Derek Rowbottom. Front row: Mary Burdin, Gordon Smith, Terry Clayton, Nora Lazenby, Edith Chapman.

Joe Bagley with his giant breadcake collects for Infirmary Sunday sometime prior to 1932. Up to 1932 a carnival day was held to collect funds for the upkeep of Pontefract Infirmary. Joe with his jam-filled breadcake was a major money maker.

Knottingley Congregational Pierrot Group outside the manse, the home of the minister, *c.* 1905. From left to right, back row: S. Cross, Mrs Heald, Mr Broadley, N. France, Miss Everitt. Centre: Mr Higgins, Mr Harrison, Mr Hobman, F. Marshall, L. Branford, Mr France, Mrs Lee, J. Wake. Front row: F. Adamson, Mrs Robinson, Mr Rider, L. Adamson, Mr Dunford, E. Arnold, Mr Higgins, Mrs Alton, Mr Everitt (minister).

The church school float at Knottingley Carnival, *c.* 1930. The float was entitled 'The Rose Fairy'. Seated on the dray from left to right are Molly Fairbairn, Ursula Backhouse, Jean and Joan Elliot, Margaret Reynolds. Mary Griffiths was the Carnival Queen that year.

Children from Knottingley Congregational church outside the town hall, c. 1905.

A mural produced for Festival of Britain in 1951 was displayed inside the town hall. The mural depicted scenes from local industries and was painted by a local artist.

A model train gives rides at the Festival of Britain celebrations in 1951. In this year three queens were appointed, the Carnival Queen Mary Asquith, the Road Safety Queen Margaret Finney, and the Savings Queen.

The mounted police team gave a display at the Festival of Britain celebrations of 1951. The police inspector, Mr Marsden, was one of the judges who chose the Carnival Queen, along with his wife and Mr and Mrs Burdin.